London Borough of Hounslow

Chiswick Library
Duke's Avenue
W4 2AB
020-8994 1008
Please telephone for
complete opening times
P10-L-2115

This item should be returned or renewed by the latest date shown. If
it is not required by another reader, you may renew it in person or by
telephone (twice only). Please quote your library card number. A charge
will be made for items returned or renewed after that date due.

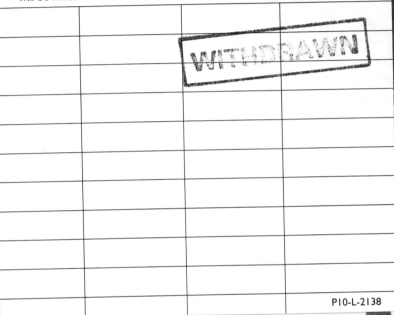

WITHDRAWN

P10-L-2138

D1437864

C0000 002 684 582

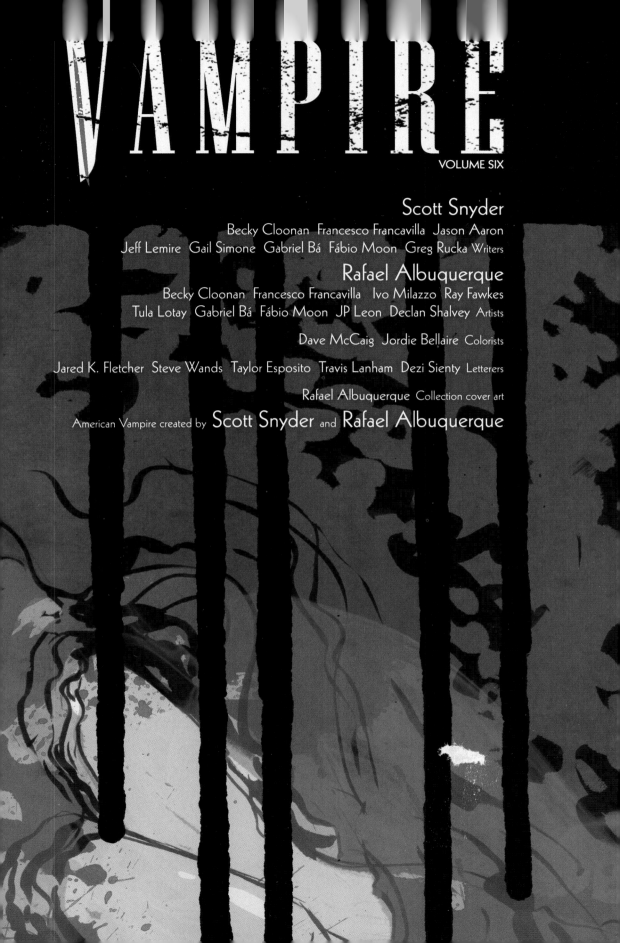

VAMPIRE

VOLUME SIX

Scott Snyder

Becky Cloonan Francesco Francavilla Jason Aaron
Jeff Lemire Gail Simone Gabriel Bá Fábio Moon Greg Rucka Writers

Rafael Albuquerque

Becky Cloonan Francesco Francavilla Ivo Milazzo Ray Fawkes
Tula Lotay Gabriel Bá Fábio Moon JP Leon Declan Shalvey Artists

Dave McCaig Jordie Bellaire Colorists

Jared K. Fletcher Steve Wands Taylor Esposito Travis Lanham Dezi Sienty Letterers

Rafael Albuquerque Collection cover art

American Vampire created by Scott Snyder and Rafael Albuquerque

Mark Doyle Editor – Original Series
Sara Miller Assistant Editor – Original Series
Peter Hamboussi Editor
Robbin Brosterman Design Director – Books
Louis Prandi Publication Design

Shelly Bond Executive Editor —Vertigo
Hank Kanalz Senior VP – Vertigo & Integrated Publishing

Diane Nelson President
Dan DiDio and Jim Lee Co-Publishers
Geoff Johns Chief Creative Officer
Amit Desai Senior VP – Marketing & Franchise Management
Amy Genkins Senior VP – Business & Legal Affairs
Nairi Gardiner Senior VP – Finance
Jeff Boison VP – Publishing Planning
Mark Chiarello VP – Art Direction & Design
John Cunningham VP – Marketing
Terri Cunningham VP – Editorial Administration
Larry Ganem VP – Talent Relations & Services
Alison Gill Senior VP – Manufacturing & Operations
Jay Kogan VP – Business & Legal Affairs, Publishing
Jack Mahan VP – Business Affairs, Talent
Nick Napolitano VP – Manufacturing Administration
Sue Pohja VP – Book Sales
Fred Ruiz VP – Manufacturing Operations
Courtney Simmons Senior VP – Publicity
Bob Wayne Senior VP – Sales

AMERICAN VAMPIRE VOLUME 6
Published by DC Comics. Copyright © 2014 Scott Snyder and DC Comics. All
Rights Reserved.

Originally published in single magazine form in AMERICAN VAMPIRE: THE
LONG ROAD TO HELL 1; AMERICAN VAMPIRE ANTHOLOGY 1
© 2013 Scott Snyder and DC Comics. All Rights Reserved. All characters, their
distinctive likenesses and related elements featured in this publication are trademarks
of DC Comics. The stories, characters and incidents featured in this publication are
entirely fictional. DC Comics does not read or accept
unsolicited ideas, stories or artwork.

DC Comics, 1700 Broadway, New York, NY 10019
A Warner Bros. Entertainment Company.
Printed in the USA. First Printing.
ISBN: 978-1-4012-4929-8

Library of Congress Cataloging-in-Publication Data

Snyder, Scott, author.
  American Vampire volume six / Scott Snyder ; [illustrated by] Rafael
Albuquerque.
      pages cm
  "Originally published in single magazine form as AMERICAN
VAMPIRE: LONG ROAD HOME 1, AMERICAN VAMPIRE
ANTHOLOGY 1."
  ISBN 978-1-4012-4929-8
  1. Vampires-Comic books, strips, etc. 2. Graphic novels. I.
Albuquerque, Rafael, 1981- illustrator. II. Title.
  PN6727.S555A48 2014
  741.5'973—dc23
                2013049635

SUSTAINABLE
FORESTRY
INITIATIVE
Certified Chain of Custody
20% Certified Forest Content,
80% Certified Sourcing
www.sfiprogram.org
SFI-01042
APPLIES TO TEXT STOCK ONLY

the LONG ROAD to HELL

THE LONG
ROAD TO HELL

Story by
Scott Snyder &
Rafael Albuquerque

Script and Art by
Rafael Albuquerque

HEY, HOW ABOUT SOME MUSIC?

SSSHHHZZZZWWWZZZ ...SO BABY JUST TELL ME WHERE AND I'D GOOOOO...

HEY, IT'S OUR SONG!

SCREEEEGHH

WHAT'S HAPPENING?! KEEP GOING! *KEEP GOING!*

YOU'RE DOING THE RIGHT THING...

klik

STOP!

STOP. THERE IS *ONE* THING YOU CAN STILL DO. SOMETHING THAT'S *BIGGER* THAN THIS SICKNESS. BIGGER THAN THIS EVIL.

WHAT YOU WERE *MEANT* TO DO...

HE'S RIGHT.

I DONT WANNA GO WITHOUT DOING THIS, HONEY.

D-DO YOU?

MORE THAN ANYTHING.

AMERICAN VAMPIRE

ANTHOLOGY

AMERICAN VAMPIRE ANTHOLOGY

WHEN I WAS YOUNG AND ORNERY, I THOUGHT THE MEASURE OF A MAN WAS HOW MANY *STORIES* GOT TOLD ABOUT HIM.

IT DIDN'T MATTER TO ME IF SAID STORIES WERE TRUE--HELL, BETTER IF THEY WEREN'T. ALL THAT MATTERED WAS THAT PEOPLE WERE *TALKING* ABOUT HIM.

IT'S ALL I WANTED. PEOPLE TELLING STORIES ABOUT ME. AROUND CAMPFIRES ON THE PLAINS. OR AT CLAPBOARD SALOONS, OVER HANDS OF CARDS. WHISPERED IN THE BEDS OF WHOREHOUSES (ESPECIALLY WHOREHOUSES).

1967. Route 77, Southeastern New Mexico.

SLAM

IT WAS MY DREAM... EVERYWHERE, FOLKS LOWERING THEIR VOICES AND OPENING THEIR EYES REAL BIG WHEN THEY SAID MY NAME, THE THINGS I'D DONE...

...AND THE THINGS I MIGHT STILL DO.

BUT THOSE DAYS WERE A LONG TIME AGO. NEARLY A *CENTURY.* THE COUNTRY'S CHANGED, AND SO HAVE I.

TAKE THIS PLACE, FOR EXAMPLE... FAR FROM THE HIGHWAYS AND BYWAYS. A PECK IN THE WALL. NOT *EVEN* A HOLE. BACK WHEN, IN MY *FIGHTING* DAYS, I WOULDN'T HAVE EVEN *HIDDEN OUT* SOMEPLACE SO REMOVED.

BUT SEE THIS LITTLE SHITHOLE, IT'S GOT THE BEST LICORICE CAKE I'VE EVER TASTED. BETTER THAN MY OWN MOTHER'S, REST HER SOUL. AND SO I SUPPOSE THERE'S PERKS TO GROWING UP.

DONE AND DONE.

FUCKER.

SEE, BUT THAT'S THE THING I'M *LEARNING* LATELY. WHEN YOU'VE DONE THE THINGS I HAVE, WHEN YOU'VE STARTED WHAT *I'VE* STARTED, SOMETIMES THE STORIES OUT THERE ABOUT YOU, THEY TAKE ON A LIFE OF THEIR OWN.

EVEN WHEN YOU THINK ONE IS DEAD AND BURIED, HERE IT COMES CRAWLING OUT OF THE GRAVE, LIKE I DID...

...EVOLVED AND REACHING FOR YOUR THROAT.

THE SETTLERS HAD FIRST COME DURING THE NIGHT, PRESUMABLY FROM OVER THE WATERS, THOUGH NO ONE HAD EVER SEEN THEIR SHIPS.

LIKE THE FEW OTHER SETTLERS BEFORE THEM, THEY MUST HAVE COME FROM ENGLAND OR SPAIN, LOOKING TO EXPLORE THE AMERICAS, TO STAKE THEIR CLAIM.

TO SINK THEIR TEETH INTO THE NEW WORLD.

COME THE MORNING, THOSE FEW WHO SURVIVED FLED INTO THE FOREST.

THEIR CHIEF WAS AMONG THEM.

WAIT. WE STOP HERE.

NO! WE MUST GO, RUN, AS FAR AS WE CAN! NOW WHILE THERE'S STILL LIGHT!

WHEN IT'S DARK, THE SETTLERS WILL COME AGAIN!

YES, THEY WILL. BUT WE STILL HAVE A FEW HOURS UNTIL THEN.

THIS IS OUR HOMELAND AND HAS BEEN FOR GENERATIONS. WE CANNOT ABANDON IT NOW.

I WILL GO INTO THE FOREST AND COMMUNE WITH THE SPIRITS. IF THE SPIRITS WANT US TO STAY, THEN THEY WILL GIVE US AN ANSWER.

AND IF THE SPIRITS SAY RUN...THEN WE WILL ALL RUN TOGETHER.

THOUGH THE CHIEF KNEW IN HIS HEART THAT EVEN IF THEY RAN TO THE ENDS OF THE EARTH... THEY COULD NEVER RUN FAR ENOUGH.

NIGHT CAME QUICKLY. AND WHEN THE CHIEF DID NOT RETURN, THE OTHERS FLED.

BUT THEIR LAND WHICH BEFORE HAD ALWAYS BEEN SO LARGE...

AAARRGGH!

NOW SEEMED SO TERRIBLY SMALL.

HSSS!

CRACK

HSSS!

HRRRRRRGH

FLIMP

I PRAYED FOR HOURS UNDER THE TREES, AND THE SPIRITS AT LAST GAVE THEIR ANSWER.

THE VERY LAND ITSELF WILL SAVE US, THEY SAID.

SO PICK UP A PIECE OF YOUR *FOREST*, MY PEOPLE.

AND COME WITH ME.

THEY KILLED THEM ALL.

THE WHOLE SETTLEMENT. EVERY MAN, WOMAN AND CHILD.

THEY STABBED THEM WITH WOOD AND DRAGGED THEIR BODIES INTO THE SUN.

AND WHEN THE BODIES BURNED TO ASH IN THE LIGHT, THEY LEFT NOTHING BEHIND TO MARK THEIR PASSING, EXCEPT SOME ABANDONED BUILDINGS.

AND A MYSTERY THAT WOULD ENDURE FOR GENERATIONS.

AND SO THE CHOWANOKE SURVIVED. FOR A WHILE MORE, AT LEAST. ON THE LAND THAT HAD BEEN THEIRS FOR CENTURIES.

PLEASE... LET THERE BE NO MORE OF THESE.

BUT EVEN AS HE SPOKE THOSE WORDS, THE CHIEF KNEW IN HIS HEART IT WAS A HOPELESS PLEA.

THE SETTLERS WILL KEEP COMING, THIS HE KNEW. UNTIL THE TRIBES ARE ALL BUT GONE AND THE LAND SCARRED FOREVER AND THE SKY BLOTTED OUT WITH FIRE. THEY WILL KEEP COMING...

UNTIL THEY'VE KILLED US ALL.

THE LOST COLONY

NEW CARPATHIA EST. 1585

END

Topeka, Kansas, 1856.

I'M SORRY, MY BABY. I WISH I COULD GET US THROUGH THIS.

I WISH I COULD HAVE GIVEN YOU A *SAFE* PLACE TO GROW UP. A PLACE WHERE YOU COULD SEE SOMETHING BEYOND THE DARKNESS THAT'S DEVOURING OUR TIME.

ONE BULLET LEFT...

I'VE *FAILED*...

Three weeks ago...

I DON'T UNDERSTAND, GIL! WHY *KANSAS?* THERE IS NOTHING HERE! HOW ARE WE SUPPOSED TO START A *FAMILY* IN THIS BACKWATER TOWN?

THAT'S THE WHOLE POINT, MY DEAR. SOON, THIS COUNTRY COULD BE TORN IN *HALF.* BUT THIS IS A NEW PLACE! A NEW OPPORTUNITY! A PLACE WHERE WE CAN STOP *TALKING* AND START *DOING...*

TRUST ME. THIS PLACE REPRESENTS *REVOLUTION,* MARIE.

REVOLUTION, HUH, MR. *JONES?*

LOOK ON THE BRIGHT SIDE...

"...HERE WE HAVE A CHANCE TO *FIGHT*."

MISTER JONES, THE END OF WHAT YOU CALL "SLAVERY" WOULD REPRESENT A MASSIVE *LOSS* FOR THE WHOLE COMMUNITY. WE ARE BUILDING A NEW STATE HERE. HOW CAN YOU ASK ABOUT QUALITY OF LIFE OF THESE...ANIMALS?

THEY ARE *PEOPLE*, JUST LIKE YOU AND ME! WE CANNOT BUILD A HOUSE IF WE DON'T HAVE A SOLID FOUNDATION, MR. PETERSON!

THIS SOCIETY SHOULD BE BASED ON *EQUALITY*, AND THE SLAVES SHOULD BECOME CITIZENS!

CALM DOWN, SIR. WE APPRECIATE YOUR *PROGRESSIVE* IDEAS, OF COURSE, BUT, COMPARING SLAVES TO PEOPLE IS *NONSENSE*.

THEY DON'T EVEN *LISTEN* TO ME, MARIE!

TOPEKA HOTEL

THEY JUST SEE IT ALL AS A BIG BUSINESS, CHEAP LAND TO EXPAND THEIR *PLANTATIONS.*

GIL...

THAT'S ALL THEY THINK ABOUT, *PROFIT!*

GIL... I'M *PREGNANT.*

P-PREGNANT?

YES. DR. COOPER CAME HERE TODAY. HE SAID I'M ALMOST TWO MONTHS NOW.

OH, DARLING. MAYBE...MAYBE YOU WERE RIGHT... MAYBE THIS IS NOT THE RIGHT PLACE FOR US TO RAISE A FAMILY AFTER ALL... WHAT ARE WE GOING TO DO?

THERE *IS* NO PERFECT WORLD, GIL. WE HAVE TO FIGHT TO *MAKE* IT RIGHT FOR OUR FAMILY. LET'S STAY, AND FIND A PLACE TO BUILD OUR *HOME.* WE'LL MAKE A *STAND* FOR OUR HOME.

LATER...

MARIE, MARIE! WE HAVE TO GO!

W-WHA?

THE *BORDER RUFFIANS* ARE BACK! THEY JUST SET FIRE TO THE PRINTING PRESS AND THEY'RE SAYING THIS HOTEL IS *NEXT*. WE HAVE TO GO!

HEY LITTLE LOVE BIRDS! HOW ABOUT YOU GET BACK INSIDE...

...AND GET READY FOR *DINNER?*

BLAM

MARIE! MY FATHER'S *REVOLVER!* INSIDE MY DRAWER... RUN!

MAKE A
STAND! MAKE A
STAND!

HOLD ON, GIL!

N-NO...

NOW

HSSSSSSS

I'VE FAILED YOU BOTH.

TIC

BUT I'LL KEEP MY PROMISE UNTIL THE END.

HSSSSSSSSS

KLIK

THE SUN...

BLEEDING KANSAS

THIS IS WHERE I'LL MAKE A STAND FOR OUR HOME.

END

YOU! *KID!* STOP RIGHT THERE!

WHAT THE BLAZES *HAPPENED* HERE?!

QUIET?! YOU DARE TELL ME TO BE QUIET, KID?!

<LOOK WHAT YOUR DAMN PEOPLE DID HERE!? WHERE ARE THE WHITE MEN?! WHERE ARE YOUR PEOPLE HIDING THE *BODIES!?* >

<MY PEOPLE DID *NOT* DO THIS. YOU MUST BE QUIET OR *THEY* WILL GET YOU TOO!>

<WHO? WHO DID THIS, THEN?! SPIT IT OUT!>

<W—WHITE MONSTERS!>

<WHAT NONSENSE ARE YOU TALKING ABOUT?! WHERE ARE YOUR PEOPLE? WHAT HAVE THEY DONE TO THE WHITE MEN WHO MADE CAMP HERE?>

<YOU *DON'T* UNDERSTAND. THE WHITE MEN WHO CAME WERE NOT LIKE YOU. THEY WERE *BAD THINGS.* DEAD EYES. DEAD *HEARTS.* >

<AND ONE BY ONE THEY TOOK MY PEOPLE INTO THEIR CAMP. PROMISING TO TRADE MARTEN FURS...BUT THEY NEVER CAME BACK. THEY BURNED ALL OF OUR CANOES. TRAPPED US HERE. HUNTED US LIKE FOX.>

<OH, AND HOW DID YOU SURVIVE THESE "WHITE MONSTERS WITH DEAD EYES"?> EH, KID?

<THE *CREE* WAY. WHEN I DON'T WANT TO BE SEEN...I AM NOT SEEN. AND IN THE DAYLIGHT, WHILE THEY SLEEP, I AM BUILDING A NEW CANOE.>

<THESE ARE THE THINGS MY GRANDFATHER TAUGHT ME. HE WAS THE LAST TO BE TAKEN. HE WAS A TRUE WARRIOR. I CAME HERE TO GET HIS MEDICINE POUCH. IT DOES NOT BELONG IN THIS EVIL PLACE.>

<WE MUST GO. IT'S ALMOST DARK! I'VE STAYED OUT HERE TOO LONG! WE MUST LEAVE THIS PLACE! HURRY!>

<NOW JUST WAIT A MINUTE! THIS IS ABSURD!>

WELL, WELL WELL...

<TOO LATE! RUN!>

WHA--?!

<WAIT.>

<SO THEN... ARE YOU READY? LET'S SEE JUST *HOW FAST* YOU CAN RUN, EH, KID?>

<NOW YOU'RE A WARRIOR TOO. TRUE CREE.>

<GO!!>

ALL RIGHT THEN, YOU KRAUT FUCKS. YOU THINK YOU CAN COME TO *MY COUNTRY* AND SPREAD YOUR DISEASE...

UNGH!-- NOT AS LONG AS THERE'S STILL *TRUE CANADIAN* BLOOD LEFT IN JACK WARNHAMMER'S VEINS!

I MADE IT TO SHORE THREE DAYS LATER. HUNGRY AND TERRIFIED...BUT *ALIVE.*

I NEVER SPOKE OF WHAT HAPPENED ON THAT ISLAND. I NEVER AGAIN HEARD OF THE MAN WHO SAVED ME. I NEVER EVEN KNEW HIS NAME, BUT HE CALLED ME *"KID".*

KID. THAT WAS THE FIRST ENGLISH WORD I LEARNED. I CARRIED A BIT OF HIM WITH ME IN THAT WORD...

...AND I EVEN PASSED IT ON TO *FAMILY.*

Canadian Vampire

End.

SQUINT

THERE'S NO WATER WITHIN A HUNDRED MILES O' HERE!

COME ON, GIRL!

POOR THING JUST NEEDS A DRINK.

TOO BAD ALL THE WATER IS RATIONED.

DRY UP, MAC.

YOU KNOW, IF THAT ANIMAL DIES, YOU STILL HAVE TO GET IT TO THE NEXT LOCATION.

MAX SAID HE NEEDS IT.

EEEEYOOORE

SKINNER SWEET STARS IN GREED

THIS SOUNDS PROMISING.

DEATH VALLEY. AT 337 FEET *BELOW* SEA LEVEL IT IS THE LOWEST, HOTTEST AND *DRIEST* PLACE IN THE WORLD.

GET ME ANOTHER TOWEL-- DAMN THING KEEPS OVERHEATING.

THE AVERAGE TEMPERATURE DURING AUGUST IS 128 DEGREES.

SUCH WAS THE HEAT OF THE DAY THAT THE CLIMATE AT NIGHT WAS CHARACTERIZED BY ITS ABSENCE.

THIS WAS ONLY *ONE OF* ITS MANY DANGERS.

ACTION!

DANGERS THAT *COILED* PATIENTLY...

COME ON.

MAX! I FOUND A REPLACEMENT FOR GIBSON! WE WON'T BE ABLE TO SHOOT ANY *CLOSE-UPS,* BUT WE SHOULD BE ABLE TO FILM MOST OF THE *FIGHT* SCENE.

WHAT IS HIS NAME?

SKINNER. SKINNER SWEET.

MR. SWEET. KINDLY TAKE YOUR PLACE BY THE DEAD HORSE.

PERFECT!

DO NOT MOVE! I WILL *DIRECT* YOU. ROLL FILM! AND...

I'M JEAN. I GUESS YOU'RE GIBSON'S STAND-IN, HUH? I DON'T SUPPOSE YOU'VE READ THE SCRIPT.

SCRIPT?

I'M SURE YOU'LL DO FINE. YOU SMELL THE PART ALREADY.

SNORT

ACTION! NOW. START TO *HATE* EACH OTHER.

PAT PAT

AND... CUT!

THAT'S IT?

THANKS FOR NOT HITTING ME *TOO* HARD, PAL.

MR. SWEET! YOU DID PRETTY GOOD OUT THERE.

THANK YOU, MISS...

SOMEBODY TAKE CARE OF THIS ANIMAL.

IT'S BEGINNING TO SMELL.

EVE MILLER.

GIVE A RING IF YOU'RE EVER IN HOLLYWOOD. MAX THINKS YOU HAVE "MOXIE."

...AND WHAT DO *YOU* THINK?

I THINK YOU WANT YOUR HAT BACK.

I RECKON I DO.

THE LAST TIME SKINNER HAD GIVEN ANY THOUGHT TO CALIFORNIA WAS DREAMS OF THE *GOLD RUSH,* BACK WHEN HE WAS A BOY.

HE HAD DECIDED TO AVOID THE STATE ALTOGETHER. BUT NOW...

NOW THE WORD "HOLLYWOOD" TASTED PRETTY GOOD AS IT ROLLED AROUND IN HIS MOUTH.

JUST GREAT. FIRST OUR LEAD ACTOR AND NOW OUR MAIN CAMERAMAN? WHO'S *NEXT!*

THIS FILM IS CURSED, I TELL YOU.

POOR MAC.

I HOPE HE FEELS BETTER TOMORROW.

IT TASTED LIKE SUNSHINE, HONEY, JUICE AND GOLD.

BRIGHT, YELLOW, HARD AND COLD. THE PRICE OF MANY CRIMES UNTOLD.

AMONG OTHER THINGS...

SUCH WAS SKINNER.

FIN

BRAVO!!!

YAY!!!

THE END

DIE, YOU BASTARD!!

CLAP CLAP CLAP CLAP CLAP CLAP CLAP CLAP CLAP CLAP CLAP CLAP CLAP CLAP CLAP CLAP CLAP CLAP

ANOTHER GREAT MOVIE, ANOTHER HIT FOR YOU, CHASE. YOU WERE GREAT IN THE ROLE OF THE HUNTER.

WELL, THEN, SWEETIE, LET'S GO MEET MY PRODUCERS.

REGAL

THE VAMPIRE

THANK YOU, MY DEAR. YOU STILL INTERESTED IN BECOMING THE NEXT HOLLYWOOD STAR?

OH MY GOD YES, I WOULD KILL TO BE IN A MOVIE WITH YOU.

"THE PRODUCERS"

starring **CHASE HAMILTON**

Written & Directed by **FRANCESCO FRANCAVILLA**

Two Years Ago. Somewhere on the Outskirts of L.A.

HOW DID THAT AUDITION GO, CHASE?

NOT WELL. I'M LOSING HOPE OF BREAKING INTO THIS ACTING BUSINESS. MAYBE IT'S TIME TO JUST HEAD BACK TO GEORGIA AND THOSE PEACH FARMS...

HEY LOOK, OUR MYSTERIOUS GUEST IS BACK!

I DON'T LIKE THIS. WONDERING IF HE IS A CROOK...

...OR A COP.

DOES HE LOOK LIKE A COP TO YOU?

I DUNNO. HE SEEMS TO BE LOOKING FOR SOMETHING. AND HE ONLY COMES BY NIGHT.

HELLO?

IS ANYBODY HE...

KEEP YOUR FANGS OFF HIM, VAMPIRE!

LET HIM GO. NOW!

OLD MAN? WHAT....WHAT'S GOING ON HERE? WHO ARE YOU?

NAME'S JEREMIAH HARREN AND I'M A VASSAL OF THE MORNING STAR, AN ORGANIZATION THAT HUNTS VAMPIRES.

VAMPIRES? ARE THEY REAL?

VERY REAL, YOU JUST MET ONE. WE KNEW OF VAMPIRE ACTIVITIES IN THE AREA SO I'VE BEEN SCOUTING THE PLACE IN THE GUISE OF A BUM...

WAITING FOR THIS DEVILISH CREATURE TO SHOW UP, AND HE FINALLY DID.

NOW STAY BACK WHILE I SEND THIS ABOMINATION BACK TO H...

THUD

IF YOUR KIND CAN HELP ME GET INTO THE MOVIE BUSINESS, I CAN PROVIDE YOU WITH FRESH BLOOD.

WHY DID YOU DO IT?

BECAUSE IF YOU REALLY ARE WHAT HE SAID YOU ARE, MAYBE WE CAN HELP EACH OTHER.

I'M LISTENING.

I KNOW HOW TO PICK PEOPLE WHO HAVE NO CONNECTION HERE, SO NOBODY WILL BE MISSING THEM OR LOOKING FOR THEM.

DEAL?

DEAL.

GOOD. YOU MIGHT WANT TO FEED ON HIM NOW BEFORE IT'S TOO LATE.

My dearest friend, Pearl.

Maybe you'll understand, pet.

Just days before we met, I was still humping roses to the powder-boy tourists pretending to be Valentino, you know the type.

ESSENCE OF LIFE

When HE walked in. Pearl, I lost the air in my chest!

AND HOW ARE YOU THIS GLORIOUS DAY, DARLING?

THE ARRANGEMENT IN THE WINDOW, I MUST HAVE IT FOR MY PARTY.

Endless cattle calls and auditions and the first real DIRECTOR I'd ever actually speak to wanders into that horrid little florist shop by sheer chance!

OF COURSE, MR. KURZIKAL! IT'S AN HONOR!

YOU KNOW OF MY WORK? DELIGHTFUL.

AND DO I DETECT A CHICAGO ACCENT? TRANSCENDENT!

With no make-up but borrowed lipstick, wearing a dress I'd found at the Salvation Army and hemmed myself...

..I met HIM. Dominic Kurzikal.

I...I SAW SHE LOVES TO MAKE WHOOPIE THREE TIMES.

I made a note to take more elocution classes.

I didn't know what to do...ask for an autograph? Perform a monologue?

I went for flattery.

AND YOU ARE AN ACTRESS, YES?

WHAT A WASTE FOR SOMEONE LIKE YOU TO WORK IN SUCH A PLACE!

JESUS. NICE **FELLA**, THERE, DOLLFACE.

They made fun of it, but it was the Chicago in me that kept me from jumping out in front of the nearest moving car.

I didn't cry. My breathing heaved like my ribs would crack.

My eyes burned so hot I thought they'd pop.

I washed my hair four times, I brushed my teeth until my gums were raw. But I didn't cry.

And I felt a new little pissant survivor inside me, in my guts, like I'd...like I'd swallowed it.

And it said, "This is your chance, idiot."

So I read the script. I couldn't help myself.

And it was...good. Subtle. MOVING, even.

"Agnes" is a tough little waitress, she tries to convince the heroine that there're no good men left.

I understood Agnes. I WAS Agnes.

And she was FROM Chicago, Pearl. Can you imagine?

"Don't muff it"?

Screw YOU, Vincent.

I'm going to be a STAR.

New York, 1940.

LAST NIGHT

"WHEN WE ARRIVED AT *THE PLAYHOUSE*, THE NIGHT WAS ALREADY IN FULL SWING.

"WE GOT IN RIGHT AT THE END OF THE HARVEST SISTERS ACT.

"THE PLAYHOUSE AIN'T LIKE THE COTTON CLUB, YOU KNOW? IT HAS ALL SORTS OF ATTRACTIONS...

"...THAT ATTRACT ALL SORTS OF CROWDS.

"THE SISTERS WERE THE EYE CANDY...

"...BUT FOR SOME FOLKS, WE WERE THE MAIN DISH."

"I WISH YOU COULD'VE SEEN US YESTERDAY, MISTER.

"WE PLAYED OUR HEARTS OUT...

"...AS IF WE WERE PLAYING FOR THE LAST TIME.

"WHICH BRINGS US BACKSTAGE, WHERE A PARTICULAR GROUP OF INDIVIDUALS WANTED TO SHOW US THEIR APPRECIATION."

"WE WERE THE CLOSING ACT..."

"...BUT THEY WERE HUNGRY FOR MORE."

"VERY HUNGRY."

OH, MY.

AND WHAT HAPPENED NEXT?

HOW DID YOU ESCAPE?

I GOT LUCKY.

"I WOKE UP THE NEXT DAY AND WENT BACK INSIDE..."

"...BUT THERE WASN'T ANYTHING THERE TO GO BACK TO.

"EVERYBODY WAS DEAD, AND THOSE MONSTERS WERE GONE."

THIS IS ALL VERY UNFORTUNATE...

...BUT I'M AFRAID I CAN'T PRINT YOUR STORY.

End.

"Portland, Oregon. February, 1940." and "PORTLAND 1940" title, and speech bubble "...I'M LEAKIN' HERE..."

"...FUCKIN' STILL LEAKIN'..."

Right panels: "...LEAKIN' FOR YEARS..." "...NOT GONNA GO OUT LIKE THIS..." and "...WASTING AWAY..."

"HEY, WATCH IT!"

"YOU OWE ME AN APOLOGY." "THAT'S WHAT YOUR MOMMA SAID..."

Bottom: "...BUT SHE ASKED FOR SECONDS." "DAMN RUMMY--"

**Portland, Oregon.
February, 1940.**

PORTLAND 1940

...I'M LEAKIN' HERE...

...FUCKIN' STILL LEAKIN'...

...LEAKIN' FOR YEARS...

...NOT GONNA GO OUT LIKE THIS...

...WASTING AWAY...

HEY, WATCH IT!

YOU OWE ME AN APOLOGY.

THAT'S WHAT YOUR MOMMA SAID...

...BUT SHE ASKED FOR SECONDS.

DAMN RUMMY--

--YOU OKAY?

NO.

LET ME *HELP*, HOLD ON.

GET YOU *OUT OF* THE *RAIN* AT LEAST.

YOU *SICK*? YOU DON'T WANT TO BE *SICK* OUT IN THE *RAIN*.

SICK... GUESS I AM...

...HAVE BEEN FOR A LONG *TIME*...

...SINCE *LAS VEGAS*...

YOU'RE A *LONG WAY* FROM HOME. HERE, WE'LL GET YOU *RIGHT*...

...GET A *STRONG DRINK* IN YOU.

WE'RE *CLOSED.*

THIS MAN NEEDS A *STRONG* DRINK, SIR.

HERE YOU GO.

DRINK UP.

NOT...

...WHAT I NEED...

YOU ONLY *CRIMPED* TWO TONIGHT?

WORD'S *OUT* ABOUT THE *SHANGHAIING.*

BEST I COULD *DO.*

JESUS, COLBY, THIS GUY'S GOT *NO* PULSE!

HE'S *DEAD!*

WON'T BE THE *FIRST* TIME I SOLD A *CORPSE* TO A *CAPTAIN.*

THEY TAKE 'EM ABOARD *DRUGGED* ANYWAY...

...WHOEVER *BUYS* HIM WILL BE TWENTY MILES AT SEA BEFORE HE *REALIZES* HE'S BEEN *STIFFED.*

HNNH

DEAD GUY'S *COVERED* IN BLOOD.

THAT WON'T *DO*. GOT THE *CAPTAIN* FROM THE *SANTA CRISTOPH* COMING IN AN *HOUR,* HE SEES THAT, HE WON'T *BUY.*

GET HIM *STRIPPED,* I'LL SEE IF I CAN'T RUSTLE SOME *CLEAN* CLOTHES.

DAMN *CRAZY,* SHANGHAIIN' A *DEAD* MAN...

...OH JESUS LORD...

...*COLBY!* THE DEAD ONE'S BEEN *SHOT,* FOR CRISSAKES!

AND HE'S *LEAKING!*

WELL, CLEAN HIM THE HELL UP, *DAMMIT!*

DON'T KNOW YOUR *STORY,* BUDDY...

...BUT LOOKS LIKE YOU DIED *ROUGH...*

TUNK

HUH...

...WELL DAMN ME FOR A FOOL...

...LOOKS LIKE GOLD...

COLBY! YOU AIN'T NEVER GONNA BELIEVE THIS!

THIS GUY, THIS DEAD GUY?

LOOKS LIKE HE WAS SHOT WITH A GOLD BULLET!

DON'T SHOUT IT, NOW.

WE DON'T WANT THE WHOLE WORLD TO HEAR, DO WE?

THOUGHT I DUG ALL YOU OUT OF ME BACK IN NEVADA.

AND HERE YOU ARE, HIDING INSIDE ME ALL THESE YEARS.

FOUND SOME *CLEAN* CLOTHES OFF ONE OF THE *LUMBERMEN* WE TOOK LAST WEEK.

HOW'S THE *DEAD* GUY...?

HE'S FEELIN' *MUCH* BETTER, THANK YOU FOR *ASKIN'*.

HE DOESN'T EVEN MIND HOW YOU TRIED TO *KIDNAP* HIM TO SELL AS *CREW.*

HE CAN SEE A *PROFIT* IN THAT, MATTER OF FACT.

HKH

HE THINKS *MAYBE* YOU MIGHT NEED A NEW *PARTNER...*

End.

AND OFF WE GO.

BUT WHAT I'VE LEARNED THESE PAST YEARS IS THAT ALL OF IT, ALL THE THINGS WHISPERED ON DEATHBEDS OR SHOUTED IN RAGE, ALL THE STORIES TOLD, THEY'RE JUST A *FRACTION* OF IT...OF THE *BIGGER* THING.

BECAUSE THERE IS A BIGGER STORY HAPPENING HERE.

SOMETHING WE'RE ALL A PART OF, ME AND *PEARL* AND ALL OF THEM. THAT MUCH I KNOW. HELL, IT'S WHY I'M WAY *OUT* HERE. TO STAY OUT OF IT. BUT SURE ENOUGH, *SOON* ENOUGH, I KNOW IT'LL COME FOR ME, TOO.

AND WHEN IT DOES, THAT'S WHEN THE WILDEST STORIES OF ALL WILL BE BORN.

THE MAN COMES AROUND

END.

SNYDER / ALBUQUERQUE

AMERICAN VAMPIRE:
THE LONG ROAD TO HELL #1
variant cover art by Tony Moore

THE LONG ROAD TO HELL

Billy Bob

Jolene

LAYOUTS
AND
DESIGN
BY
DECLAN
SHALVEY

DESIGNS BY TULA LOTAY